WRITING F

WRITING FLASH FICTION

HOW TO WRITE VERY SHORT STORIES AND GET THEM PUBLISHED *THEN RE-PUBLISH THEM ALL TOGETHER AS A BOOK

CARLY BERG

Magic Lantern Press
Houston, TX

Published by Magic Lantern Press
Houston, TX

ISBN: 978-0-692-35500-8

Typesetting services by BOOKOW.COM

Dedicated to Greg, who has dedicated so much to me

Author's Note

Like most writers, I fumbled around for too many years without much to show for it. Somewhere around, oh I dunno, my eight millionth failure to finish a novel I'd started, I happened to hear about flash fiction.

I wrote a short-short story in a couple of hours. It wasn't bad. More importantly, it was *finished*, and I was hooked.

Over the next year or so, I wrote over a hundred more flash stories and got them published in dozens of print and online publications. Some of them were published two or even three times during those months. I got some cool prizes and honors, too.

Then I gathered my stories together, organized them, and re-published them as a book. Did you hear me say I published a book? Oh, yeah! (By the way, it's called *Coffee House Lies: 100 Cups of Flash Fiction*, and is available at amazon.com).

Somehow, before you get published the gap from here to there seems as deep and wide as the Grand Canyon. But once that giant divide has finally been crossed it's easily crossed again and again.

I wish someone had told me I could reach my beloved goals in small, quick steps much earlier and shown me the way. When you think you can do it, you do it. And then it's fun.

Which brings me to the beginning of this book. Ready? Good. Let's go.

Carly Berg

Contents

A Short Introduction to Flash Fiction

What is Flash Fiction?

Flash fiction is a story of 1,000 words or fewer. That's four double-spaced manuscript pages, tops. When it became popular a decade or so ago, there were differences of opinion about the word limit. Some people said flash fiction was a story of up to 500 words, others said 1,500. The generally accepted definition finally settled in at 1,000 words.

Although very short stories have been around forever, they weren't called "flash fiction," nor were they the big deal they've become in recent years. Some people still call them names from before the term "flash fiction" won out, such as sudden fiction, quick fiction, hint fiction, or smoke-long stories (because they can be read in the amount of time it takes to smoke a cigarette).

The very short length requirement is restricting in a way, of course. And flash stories commonly are like traditional short stories but scaled down, with the larger story hinted at rather than spelled out. (Don't worry, all that pretty much occurs naturally once you've done a few of them).

But that same shortness also invites cross-overs with other forms and flat out "what-on-earth-was-thats."

These cross-overs and experimental pieces still contain a bit of story movement, some kind of change from the beginning to the end. Yet that can be all that distinguishes them from, say, a prose poem, since flash fiction lends itself to a subtle prose-poemy rhythm of the words themselves, which isn't as prominent in longer works.

Or that bit of story change can be all that distinguishes a flash story from a vignette or slice of life piece.

Finally, as mentioned above, such a tiny story can come out of nowhere like a lightning bolt and leave the reader wondering what it actually was that hit them.

The typical low time investment of tiny pieces makes them the perfect low risk form to experiment with. We'll briefly go through the alleged rules later but, well, you know what they say about rules so don't get too fussed about it. If anyone wants to argue over whether any given piece technically is or isn't flash fiction, let them. Meanwhile, *whatever* you feel drawn to try out here, you go right ahead.

Why Write It?

First of all, it's efficient. Sometimes you can write a story, polish it, and send it out for publication all in the same day. Having some published flash stories behind you is quite a confidence booster before tackling the long trudge of a novel, if that's where you're headed, or as a break from it. It's hard to get lost when you're only working with a couple of pages. And even if you do end up with an unpublishable flash story, you only spent a couple of hours on it, not weeks or even years, as with longer stories or novels.

Writing flash has an additional advantage in that it forces you to "write tight" like nothing else. With so little space to tell a story, you soon hone your craft. Every word has to carry its weight or be cut. Word flab bores readers in any type of writing, so writing flash fiction is excellent training in sharp, concise writing.

Flash fiction is a great way to get lots of stuff out there in a short amount of time. Even if you don't make a cent from it (and trust me, sometimes you won't), each little story is *free advertising*. Every time someone reads one, your fame increases a tiny bit. With many quick stories, you will soon litter the landscape with your writerly name, like free ad confetti! Most of us writers just won't stop. Let's face it, we'll be writing for life. It's much more fun to spend that time as a respected, multi-published author than stranded in newbie land. And you never know when building up a following will pay off.

It doesn't stop there. Although many publications don't accept previously published stories, some do. My stories don't just land in one place and sink. They get published over and over again, and yours can, too. That's a high return on a few hours of time.

Finally, you don't have to choose between "just" writing teeny stories and writing a book. You can do both at the same time. As you enjoy the quick successes of writing and publishing flash stories, you can be saving up copies to re-publish all together as a book.

The Flash Scene

Flash fiction stormed the writing scene over a decade ago and hasn't let up. Many prestigious publications now feature flash, when at first they looked down from their ivory towers and called it "too light" for serious and important people. I'd like to know how they explained poetry then but I'm over it, mostly.

The explosive growth of the internet is one reason flash fiction has become so wildly popular. Very short stories work well online, whereas reading longer ones on a computer screen gets tiresome (try it; you'll see). Also, people have a lot pulling at them these days, from their responsibilities to endless entertainment options. This is well beyond what existed a generation ago: a zillion television channels, the games, and again, the internet. A quick story fits where a novel can't.

Flash stories are generally considered more "for the love" than a way to pay your bills. But then isn't *for the love* the best reason of all for doing anything? Also, not long ago, fantasy novels, for example were a hard sell, as were novellas of any genre. Now both are popular. Things are always changing. Flash fiction has become quite in demand with magazine publishers. It wouldn't be a giant leap if books of flash fiction took off next.

Using this Book

This little book is arranged with the intent of getting you off to a flying start with writing and sending stories out to publishers right away. Once those basics are on the way, it moves on to discuss improving your skills. Next is help with organizing the stories for the eventual book. Sample flash stories follow. Resources for further reading are at the end.

Each section ends with something to do and something to write. These activities bring the book concepts into practice so you'll get much more from this book if you do them rather than just read. They're simpler at the beginning and get more demanding as you progress through the book.

Each of the writing exercises ends in a finished flash story. By the end of the book, you'll have over half a dozen completed stories from the writing exercises alone.

If you're a more advanced writer, feel free to skip around and take what you need, naturally.

Chapter 1 Actions

1) Do:

* Spend an hour or so reading flash fiction stories online. Find the stories from sources from the back of this book or from an internet search of "flash fiction stories." Start getting familiar with flash fiction and the markets for it.

If you like, order a book or magazine or two of flash fiction (a few suggestions are in the back of the book).

* Print out five or six stories that you especially like. Put them aside as examples to refer to later if you need help with an aspect of your own flash writing.

2) Write:

* Find a writing prompt online. Get the prompts from the sources at the back of the book or from an internet search of "fiction writing prompts." Take fifteen minutes to find one that speaks to you. Even if you have a story idea of your own for today, go through this exercise to become familiar with some sources of prompts.

*Set a timer and write the first draft of a story within an hour. Write without stopping to revise. You can do that later.

Some writers do a quick draft without stopping as part of their regular writing routine. Others, myself included, do like to take their time, mulling over every word and changing things around as they go. There's no one right way but I recommend the above quick way of getting it finished at first. It's important to get a few stories finished and out there right away, I think. That changes writing from something you take an occasional half-hearted stab at to something you actually finish, revise, and submit regularly.

CHAPTER 2

Setting the Scene for Writing

Once you get a routine going, stories happen regularly. We are creatures of habit and when your mind makes that connection between time, place, ritual, and writing, all you have to do is B.I.T.C.H. (Butt In The Chair, Honey) and stories occur. I've heard it takes three weeks to make a habit, which sounds about right to me. You don't have to do it perfectly, just work at it and don't give up. A routine followed halfway or a quarter of the way still gets you many more stories than you'd have otherwise.

The Routine

My usual writing time is at night after everyone goes to bed. It's easy to slip into that dreamy world-weaving state when it's just me and the moonlight. I have a thing for having my nails painted and pretty rings on first, too. Fancy fingers type out fancy stories (don't ask me why because I have no earthly idea). I make coffee, light a scented candle, and plop down on the couch with my laptop. Then I pick out a song to play over and over again as I write. I don't like feeling trapped with an empty computer screen, so I set up my cleaning supplies and my hand weights. When the mind gets tired, exercise the body. When the body gets tired, exercise the mind. In a couple of hours I get a lot done, both writing and my other daily stuff.

It took some arranging and re-arranging to figure out what worked best for me, and now my mind has made the connection that the scenario above means it's writing time. It doesn't matter if I'm not in the mood to write or don't think I have anything to say. Since that mind-routine connection is solid now, once I get set up to write, a story happens. I don't do it every night, usually a couple of nights a week to reach my goal, which is two flash stories per week, written, polished and submitted to publishers (there's more on publishers later).

Keep It Light

Sometimes other things do get in the way, however. I'll have other obligations or opportunities, illness, or troubles on my mind. Also, a lot of little stories use up a lot of ideas. Now and then I seem to have simply used up my imagination stores. Being upset kills it for me, too. If some big family drama is going on, chances are my creative side will go flat, and that's that. I accept it, and go do something else or nothing else. And try again another night.

Once you get into the writing habit, it's addicting and you'll probably be driven to write and crabby if you can't. But if you push *too* hard, it becomes an unpleasant chore in your mind and you don't want to do it anymore. Pushing too hard sets up a mental connection too, that of *hating to write*. Self-management sounds like it should be easy but so many of us have to work at it. If you're one of us, keep working at those routines persistently, but at the same time, not too harshly. Remember, you're someone that you like.

Other People

Other people may need to be managed as well. People can be jealous of your writing time. They may be lonesome if they're used to your company, or worry that they'll be left behind now that you're jazzed about something else. Or they might just find it hard to understand that when they interrupt your writing with their casual chatter, it's as disruptive to you as being shaken out of a sound sleep.

If it's a problem, try to get their agreement ahead of time. Go to a separate room, put a sign on the door, and ask for quiet. Set a time to do something with them later if they seem to feel left out. If your partner will be watching the kids so you can write, offer to repay the favor. If all else fails, go write at a library or coffee shop.

Someone in your life might even refuse to honor your writing time. Writing can have a strange way of making us re-evaluate relationships. Hopefully, that's a heads-up you won't need.

Chapter 2 Actions

1) Do:

* Decide on a writing goal. How many flash stories will you try for per week or per month? Take into account your other responsibilities and interests. A realistic goal is more likely to get done. You can always go over your goal amount if you get the chance, so consider setting it on the low side. Set yourself up to win.

* Read through the section above again and decide on a tentative writing routine. For now, just a time and place and one or two other details is enough. You can add and adjust as you go along. Make it cozy and inviting.

2) Write:

* Try out your routine. Use one of the following prompts. If you don't like any of them, go back online and find one you do like:

- There's a knock at your door. It's someone from your past.

- You are pretty sure something or someone is living under your bed.

- You decide to start a club whose members must have the same first name as you.

Set the timer for an hour and go!

CHAPTER 3

Getting Ideas

I don't often get a complete flash story in my mind all at once. I get a fragment, and that's enough. Add one sentence at a time, one thought at a time, and a story takes shape. You'll get plenty of fragments and they often ride around in your mind for a few days or weeks before they're ready. Trust the fragments.

When you write a lot of little stories, your imagination can run out occasionally, but overall it becomes more active. Pieces of the past emerge, ready to be plucked, twisted, and expanded into a story. Something you read, see, hear, or smell pops into your mind and you know that's your fragment for the day.

An Idea Notebook

Keep a notebook, maybe more than one. Story ideas or details can get lost otherwise. Put the notebooks where they're most needed if you can't easily carry one around with you. By the bed is a biggie. Plenty of great stories come from dreams or that in-between state when you're drifting off to sleep or waking up. Also consider keeping one in the car and in your desk at work. It doesn't take long to get a store of ideas to choose from.

Writing Prompts

I don't usually get much out of prompts that consist of a random word or two, but there are many prompts around with more substance. Take the time to find a prompt that jumps out at you. There's no reason to use one that bores you. Some magazines use a group prompt. There are a couple listed in the back of the book. If you get a chance to read one, it's really neat to see all the different things people come up with from the same prompt. If you do an internet search for "story prompt generators" there are some that will give you a type of character, scene, story problem and so on.

Music as Inspiration

I've gotten a good number of story ideas from music. I mentioned earlier that when I sit down to write, I often pick out a song that catches my interest and play it over and over. I write best when I'm very relaxed, lying down in semi-darkness with the laptop resting on my stomach. The song lyrics meld into that dream state and a story forms. I've written stories inspired by "Moon River" (so gorgeous and desolate in the dead of night), "Bridge Over Troubled Water," "Talking in Your Sleep," "Stuck in the Middle With You," "Starry, Starry Night," "All I Want For Christmas is You," and more. You can use a song title in a story if you want, but stay away from using the lyrics.

Physical Movement

Another time ideas take hold is when I jog or take a walk alone. There's something about the quiet movement that lets my mind wander into make

-believe. A moving car works for me, too. I've heard others say they get ideas when gardening, doing yoga, or taking a shower. If you get a story idea during a particular activity, make a note of it. That will be one to try again when you need inspiration.

Other Stories as Inspiration

Reading other flash stories can work well when you're stuck. Of course, we are not going to plagiarize anyone else's work. But reading other stories as a springboard for your own imagination is fine. Mark your favorites for later reference.

Other stories can be used as a pattern to help you get started. In the chosen story, say the first two sentences describe the setting. Go with that pattern and describe a (different) place in your first two sentences. If the second paragraph shows a woman saying something very strange to her husband, then you have a woman saying a (different) strange thing to her husband in your story as well. Or, have a man saying something off the wall to his brother, or whatever comes to you. After going on like that for a couple of paragraphs, your story will take off and you'll be unstuck.

When you read other flash stories (and you should) note any stories with an unusual form or type of scenario you're drawn to. Perhaps the entire story consists of one-side of a telephone conversation. Maybe it's a run-in with some sort of unknown being, or a beginning scene repeated three times with different endings each time. Don't worry, the story you end up writing won't be remotely like the one you used as a springboard.

Images

Online images, artwork, or magazine pages are readily available. Sometimes you can find a publication where a picture is used as a group prompt and the resulting stories are considered for publication. I can think of some images right now that have stayed in my mind through time, a hint that they'd be especially good prompt choices for me.

Once I saw (and held- the other senses call stories forth, too) an old photograph in a junk shop, dated from back when people still held wakes in their homes. The photo was of a little girl in her coffin. She looked about five years old and had long black hair and an angelic face. I wasn't looking for story inspiration at the time and felt like it would be strange to buy something so sad. But I wish I had bought it. A random photo you remember twenty years later is definitely story material.

Real Life

Writers may tend to be alone too much. I am. When my stories start getting dull, invariably I'm leaning too much on secondhand inspiration rather than fresh, live situations and people. While travelling, I seem to end up with strikingly new stories. Different foliage, temperature, accents, and light awaken the senses. Even a nearby change of scenery can jump-start your imagination. If your writing's getting stale, try going somewhere (anywhere) new.

And Many More...

You can barely turn around without hitting some story inspiration, if you're receptive to it. Consider reading and mixing up fairy tales, myths, Bible stories, news or science stories and whatever you see on talk shows. I have a story based on playing with Tarot cards and another based on playing the board game *Clue*. I took notes as I went along, and they turned into stories.

I've been saving up fortunes from eating at the Chinese restaurant here because I want to use them in a story, although I'm not sure how yet. And I bought a knock-off Barbie doll and it's been riding around in my purse for a while. I'm pretty sure I'm going to write a story about a living miniature person. Those ideas are still marinating.

Chapter 3 Actions

1) Do:

*Consider how you can best jot down quick notes to help in your writing. Perhaps a small notebook that fits in your purse would work well for you, or a couple of folded sheets of paper that stay in your pocket. Or maybe more than one notebook and pen set up in different areas would work better. Set it up.

*Do an internet search for "twitter fiction" or "twit-fic" as it's also known. You'll find some places that accept stories that are under 140 characters (punctuation marks and spaces count as characters).

Also, try these internet searches for more super-quickies: six word stories, six sentence stories, drabbles (100 word stories), and dribbles (fifty word stories). "Micro-fiction" is another one. There doesn't seem to be a general consensus on the length of micro-fiction. I think of it as less than about 250 or 300 words. With all of the story lengths above, when you find publications, read the other stories to get ideas.

2) Write:

*From your research above, write one or more of the following: six word story, twit-fic, dribble, six sentence story, drabble, micro-fiction. If possible, send it/them to the publication/s you found on your internet search. Be sure to follow the publication's submission guidelines.

CHAPTER 4

Writing the First Draft

I'll run through the basics of writing a flash story here. Writing the first draft is free-floaty and un-ruly, though. Go with the vision that slowly reveals itself to you rather than focusing too much on form or rules. We'll call in the editing side of the mind afterwards. There's a saying that good stories aren't written, they're re-written. I believe that.

It's fine to spend ten or fifteen minutes choosing a story idea, but then get to it. Refer back to the ideas in the previous chapter, if needed. If you get stuck, set a timer and write for ten minutes without stopping, even if you switch topics or it doesn't make much sense. From that, you'll find a story idea. If you feel too constrained on the computer, try using a pen on paper. Writing by hand seems to bring on a different mood, more immediate and personal.

The Title

A title is a first impression. It can pique the reader's (or editor's) interest... or not. Below are a few story titles. Which story in each of these pairs would you rather read?

"A Problem in the Basement" or "Bringing Back Beulah in the Bomb Shelter"

"Whiskey to Denim" or "The Break Up"

"The Cat" or "William and the Pink Snack"

It's not hard to spiff up a title. Just give it a second look before you send it off.

The Characters

A story should have at least one character (unless you're doing something experimental). Flash fiction doesn't leave room for many characters, though. It often just has one or two. More than four is pushing it, but like most cautions here, there are times when it works. By the end of the first paragraph or so, we should know the main character's name. Consider what kind of personality each character has and make sure they act and speak in a way that lines up. Can you picture them?

With very short stories, sometimes we just get a glimpse of a character, we only see an aspect of their personality. One way to make characters and stories come to life is to get into a relaxed state of mind, close your eyes, and play the story in your mind like a little movie. Can you see your characters? Are they real?

Don't hesitate to borrow from people you've known of in real life and their particular ways of dressing, moving and speaking. A fitting, specific detail or two makes a character ring true.

Point of View

Whether I'm using the first-person, second-person, third-person, or omniscient point of view, I usually don't plan it. The story comes to me the way it comes to me and I go with it. If for some reason it doesn't seem quite right, I'll try it another way at the revision stage.

If you're using first-person point of view, your viewpoint character (who is usually the main character, also called the "protagonist") uses the word "I." The first-person point of view is the closest and most intimate.

With third-person, you use "she" or "he." This puts us at a bit of distance from the viewpoint character.

Then there's second-person, which is less common. It uses "you," rather than "I" or "he/she." Here's an example of second person:

"You sneak into the house. No one is home, but you tiptoe anyway. The dog barks, and your

heart pounds."

Whichever viewpoint you use, be sure to stick with it throughout the whole story. We can only know what the viewpoint character can know. In other words, just as in real life, "I" can only describe another character's facial expressions or words, not what he thinks. I'm not in his mind, so I wouldn't know what he thinks.

Now, if you're using the omniscient point of view, you are in a sense playing god. You see and know all, and you *can* get into all of the characters' minds.

The Setting

Give us something about the time and place in the beginning as well. We don't necessarily need to know the city or date, but some idea if we're in sixteenth century France or thirty-first century Mars allows the reader to engage with the rest of the story rather than get lost and frustrated trying to figure out the basics.

Long descriptions of setting, or any other kind of description, don't fit into flash so tuck in hints instead. For example, after a character says something, have him pull up his hood (letting us know he's in a cold place). We don't need to know everything about the setting. Only enough to anchor us somewhere in time and space and what's important to the story. And we don't need to be told anything that is the usual thing that would be found in the given setting. We'd automatically assume that without being told.

Whenever possible, have your details do double duty. Say the character doesn't just pull up his hood, he *yanks* up his hood. From that specific word choice, we know he's somewhere cold *and* he's angry or in a hurry (we'll know which by the story context).

Dialogue

Flash stories don't always have dialogue. When they do, we want the dialogue to reveal something about the characters or advance the story. Flash fiction doesn't have room for idle chit-chat.

Make sure your characters don't all sound alike. We should often be able to tell who is speaking just from their dialogue. In real life, some people are wordy and others aren't. Some use big words, others have very plain and basic speech, curse a lot, or speak with an accent.

Dialogue is and isn't like real life speech. People tend to not speak in full, grammatically correct sentences, and we write the characters' lines the way they'd say them. The rules of grammar don't apply to dialogue. Using cliches' is something of a no-no in fiction writing, but those rules don't apply to dialogue, either. Some people and characters use a lot of clichés when they speak, so that's how we write it in their dialogue.

On the other hand, in real life, people tend to stutter and pause in the middle of sentences and say "um" and "er" often. If we copied that precisely, it would drive readers nuts, so we don't. Also, with accents or dialect, just dropping in a non-standard word they'd use occasionally is enough. We only need a touch of the accent and our mind will fill in the rest. Having everything spelled out phonetically was common a century ago but these days it's considered overkill.

Feel free to borrow speech peculiarities from people you've known in real life. Close your eyes and run the dialogue through your mind. Is that how people really talk? Is it how your characters would talk?

Hook

The hook draws the reader in to the story at the beginning.

Plot

The plot is the storyline, the main events of the story.

Conflict

The conflict is the story problem. It could be a conflict within the main character himself or against an outside force or person.

Climax

The story conflict leads up to the climax, the big showdown of the story, which determines which way the conflict will be resolved.

Resolution

This is how it all shakes out in the end. The resolution should come about from the story events themselves, and should tie up all the loose ends.

The Beginning

Flash fiction gets down to business right away. There's no room to fill us in on a bunch of backstory or sit through a whole meal with the family making chitchat, before the stranger knocks at the door or the monster peers through the window. Have the story begin just before that action that changes everything. Give us the main characters' names, an idea of the time and place, and start the story problem, or what the character wants. It's the job of the beginning to hook us into the story and set it up. It's about one fourth of the story length.

The Middle

We have rising tension in the middle. The main character tries to get something she wants (or get rid of something she doesn't want), and something or someone opposes her. In a longer story, there are more plot points where things get progressively harder on our main character. But in flash fiction, there may only be room for that one problem. The middle is usually half of the story's total length.

Make sure the story problem is a worthy one. Every story doesn't need to involve an apocalypse or armed robbery, but then neither would we probably want to read about how a girl really wanted a new purse but had to wait until her next payday to get it.

And, of course, make sure there *is* a problem. The main character has to want something that he can't get, and the story is about if he gets it or not, or moves toward one of those ends. Say, for example, a man sleeps with one woman, then another, then another, then goes home happy. Well, there's no story problem so the reader won't be nearly as happy as he is.

Try to write in current scenes. It's more exciting for the reader to get a front row seat while the action unfolds rather than ride around in the character's mind while he muses over it the next day. This is what is meant by "showing" vs. "telling."

Also, try to give us something a little off-beat, a little different. Instead of the expected situation, story problem and response, mix it up a little bit. Try taking your first thought and tossing it around. Rather than the usual boy wants girl, consider having him want her cool car instead.

When deciding how a character will respond to something, try forgoing your first thought and coming up with a different, unexpected response instead. Being playful like this can create a unique, delightful story.

The middle leads up to the climax, the showdown where what the character wants and the opposing force clash and it goes one way or the other. The climax can be subtle and psychological or loud and physical.

The End

Here we have the resolution, wrapping it up, in the last fourth of the story. Did she get what she wanted or didn't she? The story doesn't need a clear winner or loser. An indication that things are headed that way is sometimes more interesting. Even more interesting is – you guessed it, another twist. Say, the main character gets what he wants but for some reason it's lost its importance so the victory is hollow.

If you're not quite sure how to close the story, try tying the ending back to the beginning in some way.

Exceptions

As mentioned in chapter one, if you want to try something different, even if it doesn't fit the traditional story structure discussed above, do go ahead. We'll just call it "experimental" flash fiction.

Chapter 4 Actions

1) Do:

* Go back to a story you've written and re-write it from a different point of view (or use the story from the writing assignment below, once it's finished). For example, if you wrote it in first person point of view, re-do it in, say, third person. Note the differences.

2) Write:

*If don't have a story idea in mind, try going for a walk or using music for inspiration, as mentioned in chapter three. Or use one of the prompts below:

-A living, human head is growing in a jar of water, held up by toothpicks as is done to try to

get a vegetable to grow roots.

-You arrive home from work to find someone lounging on your sofa, drinking the expensive

bottle of wine you were saving for a special occasion. This person tells you they're your

muse.

-Pick a color. Use it as your title.

Now, write the story in three scenes. The scenes will be the beginning, middle, and end of the story, and will be approximately ¼, ½, and ¼ of its length.

Revising

You've finished a draft. Nice! It's so much easier to work when you have something to work *with*.

I edited an e-zine for a while and have also judged a few short story contests. Over half of what I received had no business being sent out. It wasn't ready. The polishing that comes after the first draft is where the real work begins. It's how you get a publishable story. A serious editing effort puts your story above half the slushpile, at a minimum.

(For those who don't know, a "slush pile" is an agent's or editor's pile of unread and not-specifically-requested submissions).

Let It Sit

Your next job is- yay- nothing! Let it sit overnight. We get too close to it and can't see it clearly anymore.

Go Over It Again

The next day (or later), come back to it with fresh eyes. You'll probably notice a couple of problems that you didn't see before. You'll be able to read it almost like someone else wrote it.

Now, print out a copy and read that. Problems that were overlooked on the computer screen have a way of standing out on paper.

Self-Edit

Now that you've edited your story from what you already know, go through the checklist in the next chapter for what you may not already know. Check your story against each item listed.

Editing Software

Also, I highly recommend signing up for an online editing software site (listed in the back of the book). There may be a small monthly fee. It's worth it. They're easy to use, too.

You plug a story in, and it runs a check on many common problems. For example, it may say you used the word "that" fifteen times, and that for the length of your story, you should probably not use it more than three times. The "thats" will be highlighted. You then go through and see if you can cut or change any of them. Also, it tells you the length of each sentence so you can make sure the sentence lengths are varied. And so on.

It's a nifty tool. *You* always decide whether or not to make the suggested changes. After using it a few times, you'll become more aware of all those little things that make the difference between tight writing and weak, wordy writing. Then, you don't make those mistakes nearly as often. Your writing is cleaner.

Just remember to not slavishly comply with the recommendations. If something makes sense and you need it, keep it. Don't twist a sentence into an awkward mess just because the editing software estimates that you used the word "was" one time more than you should have.

Have Someone Else Look It Over

Now it's time to get some other eyes on your story. See Chapter Eight for a detailed discussion of the critique process. In the meantime, try to get someone to read your story out loud to you while you listen. The ear picks up what the eyes miss.

Final Polish

Read it through one last time, then send it out if you think it's good. Chapter Seven will help you figure out where to send your stories.

Chapter 5 Actions

1) Do:

*Check out the online editing software mentioned in this chapter (see the listings in the back of the book or do an internet search). Then sign up for one of them. Use it with every story you write.

2) Write:

*Write a story using an image, such as a photograph or online picture as a prompt. See chapter three for ideas. Look around to find one that grabs your interest but don't look for too long, fifteen minutes, perhaps.

Be sure to write in the time and place you're trying out for your routine. (Continue to adjust the routine as needed).

When you're finished, let the story sit overnight. Then edit it thoroughly, using the steps in this chapter and the next chapter.

CHAPTER 6

A Self-Editing Checklist

Here are some common writing problems to check for. This list is by no means exhaustive. It's just a bunch of things those of us who have done a lot of critiquing have probably all seen over and over again. Going through this list will go a long way toward tightening your story.

Some of the issues below can be highlighted in your story, such as "weak modifiers" and "small motions." That will help you see if you're overusing them. Then, check each one and see if it can be deleted with no loss of meaning or if it should otherwise be changed. None of the suggestions below are "always." If it works, it works. But if, upon taking a closer look, it doesn't work, change it or delete it. I'll try to hit some common larger story problems first, then get to the more nitpicky stuff:

1) Too Much Telling

The common advice, "show, don't tell" drives writers nuts, because when we write we show *and* tell. Every little boring thing that happens isn't acted out; we're not watching a play. However, often newer writers tell at times when showing would be more effective (and by effective, I mean interesting). It's tempting to "tell" because telling is easier than showing. But it doesn't draw the reader in. The reader is hearing a summary rather than watching a scene unfold. Here's an example:

Telling:

Sheila was sad because Jake quit calling. She went with Trina and the rest of their crowd to a party in the woods. Jake showed up. But he had brought a girl named Amber. Sheila was devastated.

Showing:

"That'll cheer you up." Trina nodded at the beer in Sheila's hand, then turned back to the others.

Sheila drank it down but the buzz didn't cheer her up. *Maybe he already called. Maybe there's a message waiting at home.* She quit staring into the fire long enough to grab another Bud from the ice-chest.

"Sheila. Look."

She looked in the direction Trina was pointing. The fire's light didn't extend far into the darkness. "What? I don't see anything."

Trina leaned in, away from the other kids. "Jake's here."

He came. She straightened up, smiled and nodded at the others. Living it up. Not a care in the world. She reached into her jacket pocket for her lip gloss. She didn't look at him.

"Hey! Got room for more beer in there?" Jake walked behind her to the cooler.

Sheila swayed to the music, flipped her hair back.

"Hand me one first, babe," a girl said.

Jake put his arm around the girl. "Meet Amber, y'all."

So, "showing" means putting the characters on stage and giving us a front row seat to the show.

"Telling" is explaining what went on at the show we weren't invited to.

Do you see anywhere in your story where you were in too much of a rush and summarized what happened? If so, take your time and let the characters speak for themselves, on stage.

2) Low Stakes

If you feel like making excuses for a story you wrote, like "Some stories are just quieter than others" and "It's just the kind of story you have to think about for a while," that's a clue you may have been too nice to your characters. I've been guilty of this. I like my story people; I feel a little protective of them. If your story seems too mild and forgettable, write out the plot (the things that happen in the story, in order). Does it seem too everyday to you, not enough of a punch packed? Go back and make things worse. Say it's a boy breaks up with girl story. Add a twist or make it harsher. Boy breaks up with girl and runs off with her mother. Or boy breaks up with girl, and girl becomes a creepy stalker.

3) Too Long

It's hard to believe a flash story could be too long but, oh yes, it can be too long for the events covered. I must have had a dozen stories like this, where they seemed okay to me but nobody wanted them. After a dozen (or two) rejections, I revised them by cutting them way back. Then most of them were accepted. A story that seems a little weak at 1,000 words sometimes miraculously becomes a slammer at 500 words. If your story seems to lack pizzazz (or editors appear to think so, anyway) there's no harm trying a serious trimming.

4) No Action

This is why bar and hospital scenes so often make editors roll their eyes. People sitting around talking is likely to lead to too much "telling" - the characters talk about something that happened off-stage rather than do the thing in the present. Or, we get a blow by blow of who looked at who and just how they took a sip of their drink and the predictable flirty things they said to each other. If you've ever sat in a bar and watched all that, it's not that interesting to those who aren't directly involved. Hospital scenes are set up for melodrama. Since there's nothing else to do there, we get a round robin of each person's blubbering about how very, very bad they feel. People sobbing and grieving gets quickly, strangely, boring. This is probably because it's what we *expect* in that setting. If you've ever been stuck in a hospital room you know how exciting it's not.

As with anything else about writing, when it works, it works. But if your story consists of people sitting around talking, there's a good chance it's time to cut to the next scene. Move us to what happens after boy meets girl in the bar. Or give us a twist. The hospital visitor isn't sad, she's happy.

Even worse, is when we may not even have talking but we're just stuck inside a character's head as he muses alone.

Unless you're deliberately trying something experimental, give us some action and some conflict, not just people sitting around thinking or talking about it.

5) Story isn't Cohesive

Do your characters' words and actions line up and are they what that particular character would really do? Do the story events flow logically from the ones before them? I've read a lot of unpublished stories that were just kind all over the place and didn't add up. They read like what they most likely were- rough drafts. By the time you get to the end of the story, some of what you've written in the beginning and middle no longer fits. Try closing your eyes and watching your story like a play in your mind. Make sure everything "rings true."

6) Things Not Written in the Order They Happen

This is very common, in large ways and small ones. Unless you have reason not to, write the story events in the order in which they occur. That's tight writing. We often don't do that and don't realize it. Go through your story and see if everything happens in order with the larger pieces of the story. Then check for chronological order at the paragraph and sentence level. For example, have Jenny remember she has a job interview (think), then ask her father if she can borrow the car (act). Don't have her ask her father if she can borrow the car (act), then explain that it's because she remembered she has a job interview (think). She'd think of it before she'd ask to borrow the car. This seems a small thing but when it's a repeating habit, it makes the story kind of jumbled for no reason.

7) Describing Characters, Driver's License Style

There's no room for this in flash fiction especially, but it's really not good writing anywhere. The reason is because it's uninteresting. We don't need to know the height, weight, hair color and eye color of each character. Nothing there tells us about the character's personality or advances the story. Readers will imagine the characters in their minds themselves, we don't need to worry about describing how we see each character.

Also, if you've had a character look in a mirror and describe what they see, please delete it right away because that gets groans from editors everywhere. No one looks in the mirror and thinks "Look! I'm thin, with blue eyes." They would be so aware of this that for them to look in the mirror and think about it would be strange behavior.

Overly flowery hair and eye color descriptions get extra demerits. Please, no flaxen hair or teal eyes. Instead, slip in a detail or two that tells us something important about your character's personality.

"Sarah flipped her hair back." What do you get from that? Depending on the situation, that could tell us that Sarah is flirty, or snobbish, or maybe she's working so hard in the garden that her hair is hot and sweaty. Whatever it is, it will tell us more about Sarah or the situation than "Sarah had long, curly, brown hair."

"Thanks," he said, not looking up from his book. Depending on that situation, that could tell us that he's shy, intellectual, or not interested in the person who just did something for him. There's more in that little detail than "He was six feet tall and of average weight."

8) Problem Endings

Endings are hard. They have to tie up the beginning and middle, which you may have written without even knowing where they were headed.

One common problem ending is where the story abruptly stops rather than drawing to a logical conclusion. If yours does, don't give up and leave it that way. Work with it some more. Try to tie it back to the beginning in some way, something should have changed. Then adjust the middle as needed. If you can't get it, leave it alone for a while. Come back to it after your mind has had a chance to mull it over.

Flash fiction often has surprise endings but not all surprise endings are good endings. One bad type is when the reader invests the time to read a story and in the end finds out it was all a joke. When the joke's not on the main character but on the reader, you get an annoyed reader. Once I read a story only to find out at the end that we were hearing it all from the point of view of a little bird. It must have made an impression because I still remember it years later, and not fondly. Another annoying surprise is when the main character wakes up at the end and we discover it was all a dream.

And then there's the ending that's unsatisfying because it doesn't come about from the story events. When someone or something swoops in from elsewhere and resolves the story problem (deus ex machina), the reader wonders why he was asked to bother reading the rest of it. Make sure the beginning and middle had something to do with the end.

9) Filtering

"Filtering" means telling us how a character sensed something rather than just what they sensed. It puts unnecessary distance between the character and the reader. When we're in a character's point of view, we are riding around in their mind in the same way we experience the world from within ourselves. The character (and therefore "us") wouldn't think, "I am now hearing a bird chirp." They'd (we'd) think, "a bird is chirping." When we see a train, we think, "There's a train." Not "I am now looking at a train."

Here are some common filter words: heard, looked, saw, smelled, thought, felt, knew, wondered, realized, noticed, figured.

"I looked up and saw a man." There we have *two* filter words saying the same thing, "looked" and "saw." "A man appeared," tells us what the character saw.

"I felt his hand on my knee," becomes just "He touched my knee."

Highlight each filtering word in your story. Then go back and see if you can re-word the sentence with the filter word removed. Sometimes they are needed because wording the sentence differently would be awkward, and that's fine.

10) Characters Sound Alike

If two people you know well each sent you a paragraph by email and you couldn't see who sent them, you'd probably still know who had sent which email. Yet, in stories, writers often make their characters speak alike. If your story has dialogue, can you ever tell who is speaking just from how they speak or what they say?

11) Overdoing Dialogue Tags

Dialogue tags should be kept to a minimum. Even if there was plenty of room, which there's not, they aren't interesting. You'll often have only two characters speaking to each other in a flash story so we don't need a "he said/she said" after every line. We need just enough of them so we don't lose track of who is speaking. Try removing all of them, and reading your story out loud (or better yet, having someone read it to you). When you get lost, add one back in.

"Said" is the workhorse of dialogue tags. It doesn't stand out, it's somewhat invisible. We want the attention on the words spoken, not on the author intruding to tell us how they said it. Words like "shouted, grumbled, muttered, purred, inquired, stated, enunciated, intoned, replied, responded, snapped, exclaimed, ejaculated, piped up, interrupted, squealed" come across as amateurish, if used repeatedly. The dialogue itself, within the situation itself, should let us know how something would have been said. Check your story for dialogue tags besides "said." As always, don't just blindly remove them, study each one and see if that tag is necessary.

Even worse than overuse of "fancy" dialogue tags (anything other than "said") is adding on an adverb, too. If we don't need it spelled out for us that the character "snapped" when she said, "Go to hell," then we certainly don't need to know that she "snapped angrily."

While you're at it, check for tags that repeat what the punctuation has already told us:

"I-I-I don't know," he stuttered.

"I-I-I" *is* stuttering, so going on to explain that he stuttered is redundant.

Here's another example:

"I'm just not sure how I feel any—"

"And just what do you mean by *that*?" he interrupted.

In that exchange, the dash shows us that the previous speaker was cut off, so it's redundant to add the tag, "he interrupted."

Okay, your turn. Note why the dialogue tags in the following two sentences are redundant:

"I won't do it!" she exclaimed.

"Do you mean that?" Jeffrey asked.

12) Backstory

Rather than tell us about the main character's childhood or how she came to the current time, place, and mindset, put in only what we need to know for the current story to make sense. Look through your story and highlight anything that isn't in the here-and-now. If a large chunk of your story is highlighted, look for ways to cut that back while still giving what we need for the current scene to make sense. The characters' history is better hinted at than spelled out.

13) Long, Unwieldy Sentences

You begin to lose readers at about twenty words per sentence. There are exceptions, but it's a sign that the sentence may be poorly constructed. Another sign is if there's a lot of interior punctuation: commas, semi-colons, parentheses. When you read your story out loud (or preferably, have someone else read it to you), you'll hear if it flows well or not. Convoluted sentences yank the reader out of the story to try to figure out what you're trying to say. Break them up.

14) Not Enough Sentence Variation

Sentences that are too alike in length and structure lack interest, they drone on and bore the reader. Count the sentences in a few paragraphs and see how you're doing with sentence variation. If you have several long ones in a row, drop in a short one.

That is, unless you're doing it deliberately. A string of sentences lacking in variation can express drowsiness or monotony in a situation. Many short ones indicate something frantic. As usual, the thing is to become aware, to use things for a reason rather than because you didn't know about them.

15) Weak Modifiers

Check for these words, and words like them. Highlight them, then see if much is lost without each one. If not, leave it out. They are often –ly adverbs:

a bit, a little, actively, actually, all, almost, altogether, always, any, anyway, apparently, at all, available, barely, basically, both, carefully, certainly, clearly, completely, definitely, distinctly, effectively, entirely, especially, even, exactly, extremely, fairly, fortunately, generally, highly, hopefully, in fact, in reality, indeed, instinctively, invariably, just, kind of, largely, likely, many, naturally, obviously, of course, often, only, overall, particularly, per se, perhaps, practically, precisely, probably, pretty, quite, rather, really, relatively, respectively, remotely, seemingly, so, so to speak, some, somewhat, sort of, specifically, such, suddenly, that, totally, unnecessarily, usually, very.

16) Overdone Facial Expressions, Small Motions, and Stage Directions

A very common writing mistake is sharing each facial expression and movement each character makes, as if trying to give readers the same experience they'd get if watching the story on film. But writing isn't film, and reading about every little movement isn't interesting. It's like if we were informed that the characters breathed in, then breathed out again.

Most of the characters' little movements will be what we expect anyway. Therefore, there's no need to explain, except for the occasional one to break up the dialogue a bit or slow down the action. It's only interesting when it's *not* what we expected:

Expected: "Your mother's dead," he said. He shook his head sadly.

Unexpected: "Your mother's dead," he said. He danced in place, snapping his fingers.

Go through your story and highlight the facial expressions, small motions, and "stage directions" (for example, telling us that a character walked across the room, turned, or stood up). What percentage of the story is it, roughly?

Having someone read the story out loud often makes it clear what can be cut, with this and everything else.

Watch the habit of having a facial expression or motion accompany each line of dialogue. It sounds ping-pongy and strange. People don't always move each time they speak, and if they did, we wouldn't need to hear about it unless it gave some kind of information about the character or scene that we wouldn't assume anyway. We don't want our characters to twist and gyrate as if they have St. Vitus dance.

Especially watch "smiling." It's the most common facial expression written, I believe, and also the most boring. "How are you?" He smiled. "I'm fine." She smiled. It doesn't add much. Even worse, as with dialogue tags, is adding an adverb or otherwise elaborating. Something uninteresting isn't made more interesting by describing it further. Example: smiled brightly, smiled slightly, cracked a smile, or half-smiled.

These kinds of words tend to be boring: smile, grin, frown, cocked his head, raised an eyebrow, batted her eyelashes (I've never seen anyone do this, ever, by the way), laughed, sighed, turned, stood, pointed, crossed her arms, put her hands on her hips, crossed her legs.

Also, be sure you don't have your characters doing things that aren't physically possible.

"Okay. If you say so," she sighed.

No, she didn't. You can't "sigh" words. Nor yawn or chuckle words. (If you don't believe me, try it).

If you must tell us that someone sighed, it would be "Okay. If you say so." She sighed. (There's a period after the dialogue, not a comma).

Also, we assume people are looking at whatever the focus of interest is at the time. Go through your story and highlight all the looking words: looked, saw, gazed, stared, glanced, etcetera. There are often a high number of them and nearly all of them can be cut with no loss to the story. And, watch for eyes doing unintentionally hilarious things:

His eyes were glued to her cleavage.

Her eyes bounced around the room.

If you must tell us where someone's eyes were focused, use "gaze," not "eyes.

Also, watch having body parts act independently in general, or telling us what body part was used when it's obvious:

His arm reached out.

No, *he* reached out. Now, if he reached out with his toes, that's not what we'd expect anyway, so feel free to specify.

She nodded her head.

As opposed to nodding her leg? The small things add up in a small space. "She nodded" is tighter.

Try deleting all of the facial expressions, small motions, and stage directions in your story. Then only add one back where it seems like something is missing. You don't have to tell us everything, only the things that *aren't* the usual and expected thing. Use them judiciously, don't just scatter them everywhere.

17) Punctuation Problems

Here's another issue that marks work as amateurish. In the same way that "said" is the preferred dialogue tag because it's invisible, periods are the preferred punctuation because they're "invisible" too. Punctuation isn't interesting. We certainly don't want it competing for attention with the story itself. Go through your story and highlight colons, semi-colons, ellipses, dashes, exclamation marks, and parentheses (my downfall).

If your pages are marked up like they've contracted chicken pox, try to get rid of some of that "fancy" stuff. I'm not saying "never use anything but a period." I'm saying don't use anything else unless you really need it. Use punctuation thoughtfully, not everywhere. If a period will work instead, use the period. The "other" punctuation is easily overdone, which detracts from the story and annoys the reader.

And please, never use more than one exclamation mark. If the reader didn't catch on that something was supposed to be startling or amazing with one exclamation mark, more won't help.

18) Clichés

Try to find a more interesting way to say things than relying on worn out, hackneyed phrases. (Within dialogue doesn't count. A character might use a lot of clichés and that would tell us something about him). Here are a few examples:

at the end of the day

in this day and age

When it rains, it pours.

Avoid it like the plague.

airing dirty laundry

beat around the bush

All's fair in love and war.

drinks like a fish

better safe than sorry

beyond the shadow of a doubt

All good things must end.

With the speed things get around on the internet these days, I feel like a mention of "clichés in the making" is in order. New sayings pop up and by the end of the week, everyone is already tired of hearing them. Just a little something to keep in mind. Here are a couple of recent ones:

I can't wrap my head around it.

What the actual fuck?

Wow. Just wow.

No. Just no.

CHAPTER 7

Getting Published

Flash Fiction is Different

Flash fiction writers have somewhat different needs than writers of longer fiction:

*A market database service with a submission tracker is more crucial. It's harder to

keep track of stories when you might be writing a few per week rather than a few per

year. (Market databases will be covered in a bit)

*Genre is less important. There are plenty of genre markets (such as science fiction, fantasy, horror, romance, erotica, westerns, literary) that accept flash stories along with longer stories. However, there are also plenty of publications that accept flash fiction *only*. They focus on the length, not the genre. With longer stories, there tends to be more separation of genres.

*The pay and prestige of the publication for each story may be less crucial to the writer of flash fiction than to the writer of longer stories.

That is not to say that flash writers don't care about pay or prestige. But, each story has less riding on it when you have many short ones vs. fewer long ones. And, since most publications pay by the word, with flash, well, there aren't a lot of words. You may find the publishing credit (and free advertising that goes along with it) is a higher priority than getting a few bucks for the story. You may prefer to get a dozen flash stories out quickly, over having them on submission for a year or more to only the most competitive markets.

Pen Name

If you haven't been published yet, you'll need to decide what name to use.

If you use your real name, people will know you're a published author and be able to look up your work. You'll get the glory of it.

I use a pen name, because I'd rather have my privacy than the recognition.

Some authors use a combination of their real name and a pen name, or more than one pen name. They may be fine with their family and co-workers seeing the children's books they write, for example, but not the steamy romance novels. Or they may think it would confuse readers if they used the same name for both their detective stories and their young adult fantasy stories.

If you decide to use a pen name, keep in mind that it's just a screen, never a guarantee of anonymity. If you hit it big, people will probably find out your real name and even if you don't, they might anyway. You may be asked to do readings or sign your books one day, for example, and someone might recognize you. And most of us tell at least a few people what our pen name is. That means you've lost control of it. One of them could tell others.

If you want to use a pen name, what will it be? Some authors use a variation of their real name or incorporate family names that have special meaning to them. Or, you can just make a list of names and other words that you like. Play around with it for a while and see what you come up with.

Once you've decided on a name, do an internet search of it and see if you can live with sharing a name with whoever else has it, too. That could change at any time as new names show up online, but it's worth a look.

Author Bio

You'll need an author biography. These are usually sent with the (brief) cover letter and are written in third person. Just a couple of lines is fine.

Don't stress over this because it's not that important. And don't worry that you don't have anything to say. Of course you do. Everyone does. If you don't have any publishing credits or a website, substitute who you live with, what you do for a living or for fun, what kind of ice cream you like or what your favorite color is. Readers just enjoy getting a little glimpse into the author's life.

If you feel like delving into it in more detail, the tone of the bios can vary by publication (but the basic one will go anywhere). Some publications tend to have serious, business-like bios, listing education level, career, and publications, if any. Others are more fun, or even ridiculous. Many publications are fine with just about anything the author wants to say; their bios don't have a set tone about them. The best way to know what's appropriate for each publication is to read it, if possible. It's nice to have a serviceable all -occasion bio saved on your computer.

A fun touch is to have a bio that goes along with your story title. However, those can look a little wonky if the publication doesn't put the bios with the stories but instead puts them all together at the end of the magazine or anthology. So be sure to check first.

Market Databases

Using a market database was the key to getting so many of my flash stories published in such a short time. I most definitely, highly recommend using one. It included a submission tracker, which was much easier to update than a separate spreadsheet or notebook. (See the back of the book for market databases).

Some databases charge a small monthly fee. They're all simple to use. First, you check the boxes indicating what type of story you have, by length, genre, etc. Then, you choose what kind of publishers you're looking for, by pay, acceptance rate, and so on. Up pops a list of publishers that meet your criteria.

Choosing publishers becomes easier once you've gone through the submission process a few times and gained some familiarity with your markets.

Keep it Moving

Getting paid for your writing is good, as are acceptances by prestigious publishers. However, the writers I know who refuse to submit to any but the top ones in pay or prestige are mostly still waiting for *any* publishing credits at all in the time I've gotten over a hundred. They are hardly getting their names out there. So sure, try for some of the publishers that are deemed great wins. *But* don't make those the only ones you'll deal with or you'll likely get discouraged and not make much progress. Many of the most sought after markets are absolutely swamped with submissions and can use only a very few. They must turn down many excellent stories. Remember, we are working authors, not dreamers. We need to get published.

Get it written, polished, and out there, again and again. Have fun, get a steady stream of that success that makes you want to keep writing. And, keep littering the land like confetti with all that *free advertising*. The most important thing is to *keep it moving*. Don't get sidelined by insisting things must go a certain way, especially if that means they're not going at all.

Simultaneous, Exclusive, and Multiple Submissions

"Simultaneous submissions" means sending a story out for consideration by more than one publisher at a time.

"Exclusive submission" means sending a story out for consideration to only one publisher at a time.

"Multiple submissions" means sending more than one story out for consideration to one publisher.

A System

You'll soon work out your own system. Here's mine:

1) Strive to get two flash stories per week written, revised and sent out to publishers.

2) Send most of the stories to markets that take simultaneous submissions. Use the market database to find markets and track submissions. Send each

story to six markets at a time, following each market's submission guidelines. Only send it to markets I'd be equally happy having an acceptance from.

3) Put a copy of the story in my "Out on Submission" computer file.

4) As a story gets rejected, it goes out to more publishers. Update my submission tracker (on the online market database I subscribe to).

5) The first publisher to accept it, gets it.

6) After it's accepted, immediately withdraw it from the other markets. Mark the updates on my submission tracker.

7) Move the story to my "Accepted" computer file. If there's a contract sent, put a copy in this file, too. (Often the online magazines don't send a contract. Then, the agreement is stated on their site).

8) Record it on my "Publishing Credits" list. Include story title, length, date accepted, and date to be published.

9) Make a copy of the story for my "Book" folder.

10) Post the story title and where it was accepted, on my blog. Post on Twitter when it's published. Possibly post it other places under my pen name. (My social media sites are linked together when appropriate).

11) Be sure everything is backed up regularly.

12) If a story is rejected a dozen times, consider rewriting it or scrapping it.

13) Keep a computer file called "Writing Taxes." Record all writing related expenses and income, and also keep a physical folder for paper receipts. Even if it's not well organized, just keep it all together and decide how to handle it at income tax time.

If you want to try this system, set up files on your desktop, labelled: "Out on Submission," "Accepted," "Publishing Credits," "Book," and "Writing Taxes." Don't get overwhelmed. You'll get all this done naturally, one thing at a time. It becomes clear to you as you go along.

Sometimes I will send a story to a very competitive market that doesn't accept simultaneous submissions and does have a long response time. If I really want that "win," I'll do it. I just don't send *all* my stories out like that because that would definitely not be "keeping it moving." (Note: There are also plenty of publications who only accept exclusive submissions but answer fairly quickly).

Each publication usually has its writers' guidelines listed on the market database and also on its website. When there's a discrepancy between the two, follow what it says on their site. Always read and follow the guidelines to the letter. It's only professional.

Contacting Editors

Occasionally, an editor who rejects your story will give you a reason for the rejection or suggest changes. That's just someone taking a few minutes to try to help you on your way. It's *not* an invitation to re-write and re-submit it. Don't re-submit a story to the same market unless you're expressly invited to.

If your story is rejected, don't argue or ask why.

Don't send the editor a thank you email for reading your story. It's just more junk to clog up their inbox and will most likely only annoy them.

Don't bug the editor about getting an answer. However, occasionally a story does get lost. The submission guidelines should say what their typical response time is. Don't check up on your submission before then.

Don't call an editor on the phone. Editors are busy people and at this time, they're not that interested in you.

If you decide to make changes to a story that's out on submission some-where, save the revised story for the next place, should the current ones reject it. Don't re-submit the new version or email the editor about it.

And remember, when you join a writers' group, you can post your questions as they come up and get help there.

Sample Cover Letter

The cover letter for a flash story is easy once you've been through it a couple of times. Here's a basic sample cover letter:

Dear Ms. Editor (find and use the editor's name when possible):

Attached is "Catfish Face," a 500 word surreal story, for your consideration.

Here's my bio: Carly Berg can usually be found at a Starbucks near Hous-ton, Texas. Her stories have been published in *Stupefying Stories, PANK, JMWW* and elsewhere. She welcomes visitors here:

Thanks,

Carly Berg (you'd use your real name here, not a pen name)

On the story itself, put your (real) name, address, phone number and email address in the upper lefthand corner of the first page. Below the title, put "by (and your pen name)."

If the guidelines say to paste the story into the body of the email rather than as an attachment, then put that contact information at the top left of the cover letter itself.

Chapter 7 Actions

1) Do:

*Check out the market databases (see the back of the book). Sign up for one.

*If you'll be using a pen name but don't have one yet, write down all the first and last names that you're considering. Then write them out in various combinations. Decide on one.

*Write at least one author bio and save it to use with your submissions.

2) Write:

*Think of some fairy tales or nursery rhymes you know of. Look them up if you need a refresher. Pick one, and write a flash story based on it. Give it a twist. Say, Cinderella is the one who chases after the Prince, or the Prince prefers one of the ugly step-sisters. Or maybe she doesn't make it home by twelve and turns into a pumpkin.

Incorporate everything we've covered so far, for this story. Your writing routine, the revision information, and sending it out to a market.

Improving

Malcolm Gladwell, in his book *Outliers*, said it takes 10,000 hours to become proficient at anything. If you put in twenty hours per week, that's about ten years. It sounds about right to me. But, that doesn't mean you shouldn't submit your stories for publication in the meantime. Let the markets determine whether it's good enough or not.

(By the way, "writer" commonly refers to an unpublished writer, whereas "author" commonly refers to a published writer).

A multi-faceted approach hits writing improvement from different angles. The writing itself is most important. I believe participating in the critique process comes next, along with participating in the writers' forums where the critiques occur. Then there's reading in your genre, studying the craft and, if possible, getting a look at a slush pile.

Critiques

In my experience, aside from actually writing, receiving and giving critiques is the fastest, most efficient way to improve your writing skills. Let me add here that you need critiques by *other writers*. On the writers' forums it's not unusual for someone new to come in, post their work for critique, then have a meltdown over the results.

That happens when they've only gotten critiques from their mom and best friend before, and both have assured them they're marvelous. Well, family and friend connections are personal or social, not professional. It's no different from if they asked you what you thought of the quilt they'd just made. If you're like most of us, you are going to support your family member or friend and ooh and ah over their handiwork, even if it's butt-ugly, right? With other writers, it's different. It's business.

It takes guts to post your work for strangers to comment on. But criticism is something you have to get used to if you're serious about writing. You'll hear things you don't like after your work is published, too.

We don't see our own writing clearly because the brain fills in what we omit on the page. Letting our writing sit for a day or two helps with this gap between the mind and the pen, but it doesn't fix it completely. If you haven't had critiques yet, you'll see what I mean when your critiquers point out problems that you can't believe you missed.

I've learned much from receiving critiques, and even more from critiquing other writers' work. There are a few dozen common mistakes that jump out at you in neon colors once you've spotted them in other writers' work a couple hundred times. It's a real working knowledge that you'd be hard pressed to get otherwise.

Protecting Your Work

Newer writers often worry that if they post their work on a forum for critique, someone might steal it.

First, that's rare. Second, if this tells you anything, new writers worry about it and experienced writers don't. Third, what if someone did steal your story? Well, if you're reading the other flash fiction out there and they manage to get it published, there's a fair chance you'll spot it. Then, you'd just contact the editor of that publication, and they'd take it down if it was an online magazine. Otherwise, flash stories by unknown authors don't have much monetary value so in practice, you'd probably just get mad and then get over it and go write another story. If you never found out, then I guess you just wouldn't know. Having the story posted on a critique board at an earlier date could actually be your proof that it was your story.

Keep in mind this could happen even more easily *after* your stories were published. What's to stop someone from stealing your published stories and sending them out as their own? Nothing. But hardly anyone would bother because it's a lot of hard work to send stories out, high chance of being caught, and the pay is very low. It's kind of a dumb thing to steal. No worries!

Copyright

There's this other thing new writers tend to do, worry about copyrighting their work. Sometimes they send a sealed copy of their work to themselves and believe that "poor man's copyright" is some kind of protection.

It's not necessary. Your work is automatically copyrighted the minute you write it. And if someone were to steal one of your flash stories, as mentioned above, the dollar amount involved probably wouldn't even be worth taking it to small claims court anyway.

The other thing new writers tend to do is put that little copyright symbol after their name. If you're sending your stories out to editors, don't do this.

It's unnecessary because your work (in the US) is automatically copyrighted. So including the symbol just marks you as an amateur to the editor.

First Rights

If you post your story anywhere that is accessible by the general public, including on your blog or on Facebook, it's considered published and your first rights are used up. You can only use first rights once, and that's what the majority of publishers want. Nearly all critique sections of online writers' forums these days are behind a password, not accessible to the general public (people who are not members of the writers' forum). Therefore, you will not use up your first rights when you post your story for critique.

So, after you've polished your story the best you can yourself, it's time to get some other writerly eyes on it. Go on, post it on a critique board!

How to Use Critiques

Now that you've got some critiques of your story rolling in, you can go over them as they arrive or wait and go through them at the same time.

But first, say thank you to everyone who critiqued for you. Even the ones who weren't especially helpful. Other people will note your attitude when deciding on whether to work with you in the future or not. Don't argue with any critiquers (otherwise known as "critters") or attempt to correct anything they say. It's considered poor sportsmanship. You're *always* free to disregard any suggestions so there's nothing to argue about. Once in a while someone is just rude. Don't bother with them. You have better things to focus on than wasting your energy trying to straighten out strangers.

Don't expect to use all the suggestions you receive. I probably only use ten or twenty percent of them. First, save a copy of the original in case you over-correct and want to start over. Now, there will be three categories of critique suggestions. A few comments will hit you as correct right away. Go through and make all the changes you're sure of. Cross them out on the critters' copies so you know you're through with them. Next, deal with the suggestions that you know right away you don't want to use, because the critter has misread something or is just talking crazy. Cross those out on the critters' copies.

What's left are the "maybes." Consider them more strongly if more than one person says the same thing. However, that doesn't automatically mean you should change it. Sometimes critters who are unsure of themselves are influenced by what an earlier critter said. Also, when you wrote that story, you had an overall vision somewhere in your mind for it. If you change one thing, it affects other things in the story. If you're just not sure, let it sit overnight. When in doubt, leave it the way you had it.

People's critiquing skills vary the same way their writing skills do. When you get a solid, intelligent critique, make note of that person's name and be sure to critique their work back. When you post another story for critique, send them a message asking them to have a look if they have time. That way, you'll develop ongoing critiquing relationships with the writers you get the most help from.

Giving Critiques

Look at a few of the stories that are posted. Choose one that other writers have already critiqued and read their comments to get ideas for your own critique.

I like the "sandwich method." You begin and end your critique by pointing out something you liked about the writer's work. The criticisms are "sandwiched" in the middle.

Start with something like "All is just my opinion. Please feel free to take it or leave it as you find helpful." Throughout the critique, use terms like "in my opinion," "I think," and "I didn't understand what you meant here…" That maintains a friendly tone, as opposed to coming across as a know-it-all.

You can point out the larger structural problems, more nitpicky grammar and spelling problems, or anything else that stands out to you. It doesn't hurt to say what you like as you read through, too.

Avoid going beyond the writing in your criticism. Guessing at the writer's mental state, for example, is out of bounds.

At the end, close with something like, "I hope my comments helped. Good luck with it."

Read in Your Genre or Form

I've learned much about flash fiction from reading it. I've gotten a better sense of what makes a good flash story and what doesn't. Also, it's fun. After all, why write it if you don't enjoy reading it.

There's plenty of free flash fiction online. I also keep a couple of flash fiction books on my nightstand and read them before bed. There's usually a flash book in my purse as well.

It helps hugely to read the periodicals you want to submit stories to. They often have their own tone or preferences that don't always show up in their guidelines.

Study the Craft

Anyone who's reading this book probably has this one down. Studying is another way to improve your writing skills, whether by reading "how to write" books or taking writing classes, online or in person (see the back of the book for suggestions).

The Slush Pile

Delving into a slush pile provides a whole new perspective. Sometimes a chance comes up to be a first reader for a magazine. You might hear about a request for them on your writers' forum or on a magazine's website. The first readers read the stories that come in, obviously, and rate them according to criteria set by the editors. They often use a checklist that also has space for their comments. Signing up to lend a hand for a few months is a win-win. Also, writers' forums sometimes request judges for writing contests, which is a quick way to get a look at slush.

It's educational to see the stories from the other side of the desk. As I said earlier, half the slush pile stories I've seen were not even in the running. Another large number of them were just "okay." There was no glaring reason not to publish them but not much reason *to* publish them, either. They lacked "wow" factor. Buried amongst the "hell noes" and the "what fors?" you'll find a few stories that stand out and shine. All those mysteries of editors fall into place and make sense then. You get a firsthand look at what's likely to get published, what isn't, and why.

Chapter 8 Actions

1) Do:

*Check out online writers' forums that have active critique sections.

*Join one.

*Read some of the posts. Then post something on the forum section yourself.

*Finally, post one of your flash stories for critique. Critique someone else's story while you're waiting for people to weigh in on yours.

2) Write:

*Choose one of the story starters below and write a flash story:

-Write an experimental story in three scenes. Each scene begins the same. You are waiting for your blind date to arrive. Or, there's a knock at the door and when you answer it, a woman barges right into your home. Or, your boss is giving you a hard time and you consider pushing him out of the open window behind him. Make the scene go a different way each time.

-Write the steps to an everyday activity. Get a pen and paper and stop to write about it after you complete each step in your activity. For example, baking cookies, playing a solitaire card game, or paying your bills. Think about a twist as you work. Make something unusual happen during this humdrum activity and turn it into a story.

CHAPTER 9

The Book

Start a Book File

Start a computer file for your book. As you complete stories, add a copy to your file. Note where each story has been published and when, and any rights issues. For example, if your contract for a story states that you can't republish it for a certain number of months, you'll want to remember that. Also, most publications ask that they be mentioned if the story is published again. And, it looks good in the front matter of your book that others have vouched for your stories.

Before you submit a story to a market, make sure you won't be giving up the chance to include that story in your book. I got stuck on one story where the contract said the publisher could keep it for up to three years before either publishing it or returning it. They went out of business before it was published but didn't say they were out of business and didn't answer my emails. If they'd had a few of my stories rather than just one, it might have been a problem. Read the contract before you accept any deals.

Print your stories out so you can easily move them around (you should have a back up of them anyway). Over time, a logical organization for your book of stories will present itself. Don't wait until you have fifty or a hundred stories. It's a mess to do all at once, much nicer at your leisure.

A Word on Book Publishing

Fortunately, publishers usually *want* many of the stories in a collection to have been previously published. This is unlike publishers of novels, who don't want books that have been published before.

Collections of stories by a single, not-famous author are not in high demand by publishers. That doesn't mean you can't send it around anyway. Sometimes you get lucky.

If it doesn't get accepted, so what? You've *already* had many of the stories published individually by others, so you've already got that ego boost. There's nothing wrong with being a "hybrid" author (some work trade published, and some self-published).

My Story

I decided to skip the literary agents and start with small literary presses who accepted un-agented submissions.

I made a list of decent small presses, and began sending out whatever each publisher on my list requested. By "decent," I mean a mix of size, prestige, and time in the business. I didn't have any rock solid criteria but went by my overall impressions from my research.

Small literary presses can be slow at reading submissions. Some of them took six months to a year. A few didn't answer at all.

I got a couple of nibbles but no takers. It was out for a year and I'd gone through most of my list. My next options were the micro-presses or the co-ops.

A "micro press," as the name implies, is *tiny*. Many of them come about when someone self-publishes, then decides to publish other writers' books as well. The co-ops are somewhere in-between trade publishers and self -publishing, joint ventures.

I didn't think either micro-presses or co-ops had enough to offer me to make up for not getting to call all the shots and keep all the profits (if any) myself. I decided to self-publish. I'm happy with it.

Your deal may turn out differently, of course, and the markets demands keep changing, too.

Organizing the Book

Here are some tips on organizing your book-in-progress:

First, start thinking about the title. It's often taken from one of the stories. It's not necessarily the best story, just the one with the coolest title. Or, you can make up something else that fits. My book of flash, *Coffee House Lies: 100 Cups of Flash Fiction*, is just called that because I liked the way it sounded.

Since you'll be paying attention (unlike myself at the time), you'll be able to publish smaller groups of stories as e-books along the way. You can plan a batch of stories around a theme or at least notice when you happen to have written a few that would fit together. For examples, stories based on color names or love stories.

So, some of the stories will be published once (or more) in a magazine or anthology. Then, some of them can be bundled into small e-books and republished. Later, the e-books and other stories can be put together into one book and published again. Finally, some of the stories can be sent out and published in magazines and anthologies even after the book comes out. That's a lot of mileage for stories that only took you a few hours each to write.

You'll want to put thought into how your book is organized. If you don't do the collection of separate e-books, and use those as sections of your larger book, you may want to actually split up similar stories. That way, readers get a variety as they go through the book rather than, say, three in a row where someone dies or gets divorced.

Put the very best story first. Then keep piling on those best of the best stories. Hide the lesser ones in the middle, with an occasional star to brighten them up and keep people reading. Be sure to end on a high note. First and last impressions carry more weight, I think. However, there will probably be some stories that you just aren't proud of. We all have a few out there that seemed fine at the time but now make us cringe. Don't include those in the book.

I divided mine into three parts, by length. I've heard that's a no-no, but it annoys me when I read a collection with all different lengths randomly placed throughout the book. To me, it looks messy. I'm probably wrong. Anyway, the first part is "Coffee House Lies." It's standard length flash stories. Next is "Expresso Shots." That's micro-fiction, under 250 or 300 words each. At the end is "Free Refills," which are a little longer than 1,000 words. The very last story is standard flash length, though. I included it because it's titled "Season Finale" and ends with a slamming shut of curtains, which I thought was kind of a snappy ending to the book.

Starting early gives you plenty of time to end up with a book you're happy about, without getting overwhelmed by it.

More Editing

When I put the stories together, there were problems with them as a group that weren't there when they were singles. You have to edit yet again, this time to make sure the stories hang together well.

For example, check that you don't accidentally have characters with the same names in different stories. I found a lot of characters named Ted. I have no idea why. I don't even know anyone named Ted. Readers might easily think the same character was appearing throughout the book and be confused when he was completely different each time.

Watch for pet words. I didn't know I used "Whoopie" so much until I read the stories as a collection. How embarrassing.

And, watch for recurring themes. I didn't realize some of those, either, until a critique noted that I had repeating themes of reality television, crazy love, and people as animals. I split those up throughout the book so readers wouldn't feel like they were too much reading the same story in different words. (Note: A book of stories by multiple authors is commonly called an "anthology." A book of stories by one author is called a "collection.")

Chapter 9 Actions

1) Do:

*Start a file for your book of flash stories, as discussed in this chapter. Work with it along the way so that when it's reached an adequate length, most of the work will already be done.

*Set up an author site or blog if you don't have one yet (see the back of the book for help). You can put links to your published stories here, post about the writing life, and so on. If you don't have much to include yet, that's fine. Even "Your Name, Author" and "Coming Soon" is a start. Once you have some entries there, be sure to link it to your other accounts if they're under the same name as your writing. For example, your Twitter, Facebook, and writer's forum profile.

*If you plan to look for an agent or publisher once your book of flash stories is finished, start researching them now to see which ones consider short story collections. Make a list.

A literary agent is typically needed to approach the big publishers, they don't usually take submissions directly from the author. The smaller publishers are more likely to accept submissions directly from the author. They'll state their preferences in their guidelines.

*If you think you'll self-publish it, begin looking into that. Beware of expensive vanity presses that masquerade as trade publishers. Do an internet search on the company name and pay close attention if there are many complaints, or if you don't find anything at all about them.

*Also worth looking into, small literary presses and university presses often hold annual contests for story collections and include publication as part of the prize. (See the back of the book for resources).

2) Write:

*Go out for some real life story inspiration. Just sitting at a coffee shop with other people in it might work. Watch people. Listen to them. Imagine what they just might be up to. Or try for somewhere more unusual. Go sit in a hospital E.R. waiting room, traffic court, or the lobby of an upscale hotel. Make sure you have something to write with and a cover story if you'll be embarrassed to be asked why you're there.

CHAPTER 10

The End (And the Next Beginning)

So. Here you are, on the other side at last. You've got some stories written, some publishing credits, and maybe even a book out already.

What's next? It might be writing more flash fiction or branching out to longer forms of fiction or nonfiction. Go wherever your wild mind desires, or go after the cash with a commercially minded project. Further study, or maybe even some teaching.

Whatever direction you decide on next, now you'll go as a decently established author, with the confidence and respect that goes along with accomplishment. Congratulations. You've earned it.

Selected Flash Stories

Here are a few examples of flash stories. These are mine but you can find them online by many other authors as well:

Rush

Rush had a black eye and a bucket of dirty water. Look, a baby turtle he said, like that explained everything. Yes, I did lack a turtle so thank you for disappearing for three months and returning with a goddamned turtle. His weird homecoming gift took my focus off him while he slipped back into my life. Last time he brought me a box of brass kaleidoscopes.

This was no aquarium slider but a giant sunflower seed with a large head and large flippers. He called it a leatherback. Google search: *Endangered sea turtle. Average adult size 850 pounds.* Exhaustion overcame me. I said I need a nap.

What about us he said as if I was the one who. I rose from the table. You're pregnant! His eye opened wide, just the one. The other was swelled shut and even darker when he went pale.

For once I got to be the one to drop a bomb on him. If you could call it that considering. Still I said how do *you* like it. He said huh?

I woke to. This way, that way, over, and oh my god not that yes that. I had to get rid of him for good again. But his thick motion floated me on hot clouds screaming for mercy don't stop.

He slammed the bed 'til the bolt popped, tipping that whole corner to the floor. The rest of the bed slanted ceilingward. He didn't stop.

The next time I woke angled, head down on the sweaty Rush-ravished sheets. He wanted to go to the beach. I grabbed the bucket and glared when he opened his mouth.

Once freed, the hatchling struggled through the sand toward pink sunset and silver waves. A hawk circled above, pounced, soared. The oversized flippers swam in the air.

Someone played "Papa Was a Rolling Stone" over the surf's white noise. Our baby kicked.

Rush watched a beach-ball colored kite sail the skies. Do you wish you were up there dear, do you want to fly?

More than anything he said.

* * *

340 words. *Bartleby Snopes*, December 2012. Reprinted in *Coffee House Lies: 100 Books of Flash Fiction* by Carly Berg, 2014.

With this story, I wanted to experiment with dropping the dialogue quotation marks. I think it adds to the sense of the main character being on the ragged edge, almost like this poor lady is too wrung out to separate her words from her thoughts. It was nominated for the 2013 Pushcart Prize.

The Horse Head Earrings

Venetia Favaloro's old maid sister, Luisa, was furious when her mother died in 1925 and left the horse head earrings to Venetia.

Venetia was relieved when Luisa stopped speaking to her. Venetia, with many children and few lira, lacked energy for Luisa's nattering. Venetia envisioned easier lives for her children. As her two prettiest daughters came of age, she mailed them to bridegrooms in shining America.

Upon Venetia's death in 1946, each daughter received an envelope from Sicily. Nothing fancy, just keepsakes that Venetia's own mother had left to her. The onyx bracelet went to Antonietta in New York. The horse head earrings, to Annuzziata in St. Louis.

When Luisa heard, she had a nephew drive her, at top speed, to the village telephone. She dialed Annuzziata in America. "I command you to send me those earrings. Mamma had promised them to me," she said in Italian, crossing her fingers to excuse the bugia (fib).

"You shan't have them," Annuzziata replied.

Upon Annuzziata's death in 1968, her daughter, Carlina, moved into the house. The phone rang right away.

"I want those horse head earrings with the garnet eyes," someone warbled on the phone in broken English. "I simply must have them."

"You mayn't have them," Carlina said, having been warned that Luisa would call. "Absolutely not."

Carlina died in 1987. Carlina's daughter, Samantha, and her family, moved into the house. The phone rang as she carried boxes in.

"I want those earrings," someone at the other end hissed. "I require them immediately."

"Nope. Ain't happening, Luisa." Samantha hung up.

In 2011, Samantha passed away. Her daughter, Amber, was clearing out the house when the phone rang.

"Horse head earrings," the voice croaked. "Gimme."

Amber had often repeated the horse head earring story in bars, causing everyone to howl with laughter. "Sure. Okay," she said.

A nurse named Nina got on the phone and gave the address of a rest home near Sicily. Amber wrapped them and dropped them off at the post office the next day.

Three weeks later, Nurse Nina delivered the package to Luisa. She helped her tear off the brown parcel paper. Underneath, the box was beautifully gift-wrapped and tied with bright ribbons.

"Grazie! Grazie Dio! Finalmente!" Luisa snatched the package away, and began thanking the saints individually, in between wild whoops. When she progressed to wailing and pounding her wheelchair tray, Nurse Nina had to give her a sedative. Luisa was quite frail, as expected at 146 years old.

The old woman slipped into a deep sleep and from there into the next life, clutching the colorfully covered prize.

That's what she was waiting for. The nurses agreed. After some deliberation, they decided to unwrap the package.

The earrings were ugly. Enormous dangling jackass heads with embellished nostrils and seedy red eyes.

They didn't laugh until they cried yet. Not next to the body.

* * *

500 words. *Untoward Magazine*, October 16, 2012. Reprinted in *Nazar Look: Looking Back Anthology,* 2013. Reprinted in *Coffee House Lies: 100 Cups of Flash Fiction* by Carly Berg, 2014.

This story was inspired by a funny real life incident in which a friend of mine was in a tiff with an elderly relative over a pair of (ugly) inherited earrings.

Crimson and Clover

Baby hair stuck up through the mulch, feathery blond tufts, *dammit*. Millie tossed her rose

clippers down and yanked him out of the ground like a turnip. The boy remained still and gray

even after the mud was scooped from his mouth. But when she snipped the roots, freeing the

carcass for the trash can, he howled like a storm.

In the kitchen, the greedy thing drank half a bottle of liquid houseplant food from the dropper.

She lay him in an inch of water in the sink to keep him moist. He kicked his twiggy legs.

Bring me a big flowerpot, would you? she called to Jack, since by then she was thawing

ground beef in the pan.

Christ on a cracker, Millie. Not another one.

What do you want me to do about it? she said. She'd told him the place was built on the old

Woodstock field but he just had to have it anyway.

Dirty hippies, he said as if reading her mind.

You got that right. See if there's any more potting soil out there too, would ya?

Jack potted the new dirt baby while Millie fixed Hamburger Helper.

Late nights, they sneak a few babies onto the neighbors' porches.

They awake to a few of the neighbors' babies on theirs.

The little ones need their soil changed often and to be fed by hand. The older ones hop

around the garden nibbling the plants down to nubs with their lipless mouths. They howl when

they're hungry. They're always hungry. They give no love. It's all me, me, me.

* * *

250 words. *Apocrypha and Abstractions*, March, 2013. *Body Parts Magazine, Issue One:* , October, 2013. *Coffee House Lies: 100 Cups of Flash Fiction* by Carly Berg, 2014. *Bete Noire*, Issue #19, April, 2015.

This one was inspired by the song of the same name. I wanted to show you here how much exposure you can get for a couple of hours' time. Within two years, this one page micro-fiction has already been published five times (including its inclusion here). And I don't see any reason it would end there. I think it's kind of a weird and fun little story but I doubt it's anything anyone reading this book couldn't match. It just takes a little work and a little know-how to keep those stories out there advertising for you.

The Imago

The sun rose daily but Lei did not. She lay on her sleep mat midday same as midnight, facing the clay wall of the hut. It was her sixth loss. Lei no longer cared that the other village women saw her cooking fire cold. Or that they knew she brought no water from the river, shaped no pots, gathered no cassava. She simply waited to die.

Her mate, Mep, took pity on her. He squeezed her hand, and brought the sybil one more time. A child spirit leaves when it is not welcome, said the sybil, as before. You must start over. Make the holy image, and pray.

Lei turned back to the wall and prayed to die.

The next day, though, she did as she was told. Her heart was numb, but it was her duty since Mep had given her another chance. Lei's fingers knew clay and her holy imagos made the other women gasp. The thumb-sized clay baby looked real. A plump, curly-haired son, each fist the size of a sagudana pearl yet each fingernail perfect, thumb in his mouth for comfort.

#

She buried the imago infant among the banana trees at the next new moon, as Sybil always instructed. She left her prayers and her pure white offering, a sprinkling of manioc and tiny snail shells. Only the shiniest were fit for the Gods.

Lei rejoined the living, but as one marching toward the final peace of the funeral pyre.

One evening after market day, she returned to the hut weary from minding her pottery stall. She dared a shard of hope that the child spirit returned, and rolled the sleep mat out early. As she unrolled the bedding, a hair ornament fell out. The sybil's hair bauble, on the day Lei's mate was left home alone. The bamboo trinket clacked on the clay floor and shattered Lei's mind.

Buried. The sybil had her bury the imagos. The symbol stands for the thing, Sybil always said. The thing buried imagos stood for was...buried babies.

Lei rushed to the banana trees and dug up the imago. She took the path home past the baker's oven, and tossed the sybil's hair ornament into the fire. The symbol stood for the thing. Burn, she-devil.

At home, she placed the imago embryo in the cradle and covered it with one thin-pulled cotton boll.

The next time, the seventh time, the child spirit stayed. On the sleep mat in childbirth, a vision came to Lei—the sybil burst into flame.

Her son was born, black hair in ringlets.

He wailed. The sybil screeched in Lei's mind, the terrible shrieking of jackals ripping a hyena.

The next day, Lei's mate told her the sybil had turned blood red with fever and died. How could that be, she said. How could that be.

#

Mep was as enamored with Lei now as on their first shy embrace. He fanned her with the palm frond and held water to her lips. He murmured my beloved, my only, my pet.

But his place in her heart had cooled smooth as ash. She squeezed his hand, though, taking pity on him still. She smiled sweetly, as he smiled sweetly, at the baker's infant son.

* * *

550 words. *Niteblade*, Summer, 2013. *Coffee House Lies: 100 Cups of Flash Fiction* by Carly Berg, 2014.

This one has a fable-like feel to it, and is also an example of the twist endings flash fiction is known for. I got the idea for it after watching a documentary about a third world village.

Calliope: A Tale of Writerly Suffering

The story wasn't happening. My muse was gone. *Empty page, empty head. Empty rolled over*

and the story was dead. Empty dempty sat on a wall, had a great fall… "Calli!" I yelled. "Where

the hell are you?"

I opened my bedroom door. Calli's cigarette smoke wafted out. Cosmetics and clothes (mine)

littered the bed and what used to be my husband's dresser before he ran off with a Baptist prude

last spring.

"Calliope. I have been waiting for you at the goddamned computer for four hours!"

She sat at the dressing table, twirling my big pink pearls, which I didn't say she could wear.

She said, "Lunch, Carly dahling!"

I wanted to rip that ridiculous gold tiara off her head. The feathers, too.

She applied (my) red lipstick, admiring herself in the mirror, ignoring my murderous glare.

I needed her and she knew it. The story had to get done. "So, that's how you're going to be

today, I see. Well, no lunch. I'm meeting Linda for lunch today."

"I shall come along."

I did not recall inviting her.

"And not that dreadful peasant buffet, dahling. Alexander the Great's," Callie said.

The story, the story. On the phone: "Linda? Is Alexander the Great's all right instead?"

#

The waiting area was packed. Calli breezed past the hostess stand to an empty booth.

"Could you please wait to be seated?" the hostess called after her.

Callie slid into the booth and swooned dramatically, head down on the table, arms spread out.

Restaurant staff gathered around the medical emergency. "Crackers," she whispered. "Please.

And an iced ouzo. Two sugars."

Linda looked furious. She wasn't the tolerant sort.

I decided to hide out in the restroom. When I dared come out Callie and Linda sipped their drinks in the booth. Calli enjoyed a pillow behind her head and a blanket across her lap.

Giving up on finding something I recognized on the menu, I sipped my drink. I'd just have

Callie's dinner salad, she never bothered with it. She ordered the lamb -stuffed grape leaves,

pricey for lunch, but of course she wouldn't be paying for it.

"So anyway," Linda said, "Let me fill you in on the squabble you missed at writing group last

night. Someone blubbered about her writer's block and then the rest of them started whining too.

Their motivations were gone, their muses were gone, blah, blah blah. I said it like it was. I said,

'That muse nonsense doesn't exist. Honestly you're all just being lazy.' Then, they all turned on

me–"

"Peep!" Calli shrieked, eyes wide. "Peep! Peep! Peep!"

She was a startled tropical bird, with the peacock plumage around her crown and her bright

floral muumuu. When anyone annoyed Calli, she peeped in their faces. She really was quite rude.

I tried to stop laughing.

"Oh, just fuck off." Linda tossed a twenty on her napkin and flounced out.

"Are you happy now?" Calli usually made fun of all my friends and husbands (four). I think

she was jealous of them and wanted me all to herself.

"Boring, boring poseur. She'll never get published. Why in the world do you put up with her,

dahling?"

Callie polished off Linda's lunch as well as her own. "This moussaka is divine."

"When we get home, I need your help. I have to fin—"

"Peep!"

Sometimes I hated her.

#

Back at my apartment, Calli insisted on watching *Dr. Phil*, then two episodes of *Hoarders.* I typed and deleted, then typed and deleted some more.

She claimed she required a raspberry lemoni to help her get into the right frame of mind to

help me. I had to run to the store for the fresh berries. When I finally had her fancy cocktail

prepared, she was gone.

I found her at the complex swimming pool, entertaining a suitor, swimming in her muumuu.

She had the nerve to tell me to go fetch him a drink, too.

Dinner was leftover Pizza Hut.

She slipped out again after her second slice of pizza. No doubt for a night on the town with

her new friend. My dressy red sandals and matching evening bag were missing.

Type, delete. Type, delete. I was getting nowhere.

#

"My poor dahling. Falling asleep at your desk on a Saturday night. You should get back out there! Meet handsome men, have fun."

"It's two in the morning. I'm never going to finish this story."

"Tsk-tsk, you worry too much. Make a pot of coffee and let me slip out of these dreadful

shoes. Then we'll see."

Coffee in hand, Calli said, "It's simple, dahling. Let's start with your day. Type out what

you did today."

Empty page, empty head. Empty rolled over and the story was dead. Empty dempty sat

on a wall, had a great fall… "Calli!" I yelled. "Where the hell are you?"

I opened my bedroom door, Calli's cigarette smoke wafted out. Cosmetics, and clothes (mine)

littered the bed and what used to be my husband's dresser before he ran off with a Baptist

prude last spring.

"Calliope. I have been waiting at the goddamned computer for three hours!"

She sat at the dressing table, twirling my strand of big pink pearls I didn't say she could

wear. She said, "Lunch."

I wanted to rip the ridiculous gold tiara off her head. The feathers, too.

Ah, my muse was back! Later, I wouldn't believe I had written it. Of course, I hadn't. My

muse wrote it. I only maneuvered my muse into writing it.

She applied (my) red lipstick, admiring herself in the mirror, ignoring my murderous

glare. I needed her and she knew it. The story had to get done. "So, that's how you're going to

be today, I see. Well, no lunch. I'm meeting Linda for lunch."

"Excuse me. Did you say you 'wanted to rip the ridiculous gold tiara off my head?'"

"I'm sorry! I—"

"Peep! Peep!"

I slammed my head down on the keyboard, which wrote: frawir5h4qh46ngoagnf8

#

When Calliope peeps and I bang along on my desk with my head, the rhythm is nice. It's the

same rhythm I use when I type out a story.

This is how a writer suffers for art. And only the luckiest of us get a muse at all.

* * *

1,000 words. *Foliate Oak*, March, 2013. *Coffee House Lies: 100 Cups of Flash Fiction* by Carly Berg, 2014.

With this one, I was playing with the idea of going through a whole day a second time, *Groundhog Day* style. Don't be afraid to break the alleged rules. Trying new things in your writing is exciting, and there's nothing lost if it doesn't work out.

For Further Reading

Books of Flash Fiction

Coffee House Lies: 100 Cups of Flash Fiction by Carly Berg. South Coast Books, 2014.

Flash Fiction: 72 Very Short Stories, edited by James Thomas, Denise Thomas, and Tom Hazuka. W.W. Norton, 1992.

Flash Fiction Forward: 80 Very Short Stories, edited by James Thomas and Robert Shapard. W.W. Norton, 2006.

Sudden Flash Fiction Youth: 65 Short-Short Stories, edited by Christine Perkins-Hazuka and Tom Hazuka. Persea, 2011.

The Pearl Jacket and Other Stories: Flash Fiction from Contemporary China, edited by Shouhua Qi. Stone Bridge Press, 2008

*I found the earnestness, the complete absence of snark in this Chinese anthology surprising and refreshing.

Flash Fiction Instruction

The Rose Metal Press Field Guide to Writing Flash Fiction: Tips from Editors, Teachers, and Writers in the Field, edited by Tarah L. Masih.

*This wonderful book is divided into a couple dozen sections, each written by an accomplished flash fiction author. A flash story is included to illustrate the lesson, followed by a related assignment. If you do all of these, you'll learn all kinds of neat things and have over two dozen completed flash stories by the end.

Free Three Week Flash Fiction Class (online)

http://howtothinksideways.com/shop/free-three-week-flash-fiction-class/

*Free short online writing class by Holly Lisle, to complete at your own pace. Her technique shows you how to plan out and finish a small collection of related flash stories all at once. She then suggests you self-publish them as a group on Amazon for 99 cents (if you don't want to send them out to the various magazines and anthologies).

Flash Fiction Chronicles (online articles, flash fiction markets, and more)

http://www.everydayfiction.com/flashfictionblog/resources/

A Few Free Flash Fiction Reads Online (some of these include longer fiction and poetry, too)

Daily Science Fiction

http://dailysciencefiction.com/

*Sign up to get a story a day sent to your email address

Every Day Fiction

http://www.everydayfiction.com/

*Sign up to get a story a day sent to your email address

Flash Fiction Online

http://flashfictiononline.com/main/

Frigg

http://www.friggmagazine.com/

NANO Fiction

http://nanofiction.org/

*Also has writing prompts on the site

SmokeLong Quarterly

http://www.smokelong.com/

Stupefying Stories Showcase

http://stupefyingstories.blogspot.com/

Vestal Review

http://www.vestalreview.org/fiction/lover/

Word Riot

http://www.wordriot.org/

General Writing Resources

The Artist's Way: a Spiritual Path to Higher Creativity, Julia Cameron. Jeremy P. Tarcher/Putnam, 2002.

Bird by Bird: Some Instructions on Writing and Life, Anne Lamott. Anchor, 1995

On Writing: A Memoir of the Craft, Tenth Anniversary Edition, Stephen King. Scribner, 2010.

Self-Editing for Fiction Writers, Second Edition: How to Edit Yourself into Print, Renni Browne and Dave King. Harper Collins, 2010.

Terrible Minds (Chuck Wendig's blog- for Adults Only)

http://terribleminds.com/

Wild Mind: Living the Writer's Life, Natalie Goldberg. Bantam Books, 1990.

Writing Down the Bones: Freeing the Writer Within, Natalie Goldberg. Shambhala Publications, 2010.

Grammar

Daily Writing Tips (sign up to get a daily grammar tip by email)

http://www.dailywritingtips.com

Eats, Shoots and Leaves: The Zero Tolerance Approach to Punctuation, Lynne Truss, Gotham Books, 2003.

Manuscript Formatting (free online resource)

William Shunn's Proper Manuscript Formatting- Short Story

http://www.shunn.net/format/story.html

Online Writers' Forums and Critique Boards

Absolute Write

http://www.absolutewrite.com/forums/

Critique Circle

http://www.critiquecircle.com/

Litreactor

http://www.critiquecircle.com/

Scribophile

http://www.scribophile.com

Online Editing Software

AutoCrit

https://www.autocrit.com/

ProWritingAid

http://prowritingaid.com/

Market Databases

Duotrope

https://duotrope.com/

Ralan's (Market Listings only, for Speculative Fiction and Humor)

http://www.ralan.com/

Submission Grinder

http://thegrinder.diabolicalplots.com/

Writing Prompts

Story A Day

http://storyaday.org/

*Sign up for writing prompts delivered to your email address

The First Line Magazine

http://www.thefirstline.com/

*This magazine is based on writing prompts.

Thema

http://themaliterarysociety.com/

*Here's another magazine whose issues are based on their writing prompts.

Writer's Digest online prompts

http://www.writersdigest.com/prompts

*This site also includes a bunch of other good writerly stuff.

Setting Up an Author Site or Blog

Blogger

https://www.blogger.com/features

Weebly

http://www.weebly.com

Agents and Book Publishers

Guide to Literary Agents, Chuck Sambuchino, Writer's Digest Books (annual).

Poets and Writers online (Book Publishers)

http://www.pw.org/small_presses

QueryTracker (Agents and Book Publishers)

http://www.querytracker.net/

Writer's Market

http://www.writersmarket.com/

Watchdogs for Literary Scams

Preditors and Editors

http://pred-ed.com/

Printed in Great Britain
by Amazon